EASINGTON
THROUGH THE YEARS

BY EILEEN HOPPER

Easington Colliery Senior Girls Class 9 in 1919. Hilda Welsh (née Clark) is fourth from the left, back row.

Previous page: Final days at Easington Colliery: W. Gibson (Overman), R. Anderson, J. Dean (Deputy), R. Robson, T. Davies.

Front cover: Easington Village Green with the signposts when the old A19 crossed. All the old houses were still round the perimeter.

Seaside Lane with shops on one side, the left hand side has yet to be built on.

Back cover: An old photo of Easington Colliery pit the first coal was brought to the surface in 1910.

Villagers enjoy maypole dancers on the Village Green in June 1953 for Queen's Coronation.

Copyright Eileen Hopper 2011

First published in 2011 by

Summerhill Books
PO Box 1210, Newcastle-upon-Tyne NE99 4AH

Email: summerhillbooks@yahoo.co.uk

www.summerhillbooks.co.uk

ISBN: 978-1-906721-42-8

The publisher would like to thank George Nairn for his help with this book.

No part of this publication may be reproduced, stored in a mechanical retrieval system, or transmitted, in any form or by any means, electronic, mechanical, photocopying, recording or otherwise, without prior permission of the author.

CONTENTS

Introduction	4
Old Easington	5
Easington – The Changes	7
Easington Colliery	14
Durham Big Meeting	20
Easington Mining Disaster	22
Schools	26
Sport	36
Pastimes	40
The Churches	45
Work and Families	49
The Second World War	55
Welfare Hall	56
Health & Elderly	58
Workhouse & Hospitals	59
Women	62
Turning the Tide	64
Village Show & Fair	67
People	70
The Fame Game	74
Easington Saga in Verse	77
Acknowledgements	80

INTRODUCTION

Why has a woman born in Sunderland taken it upon her self to write not only one book in 1996 but a second book in 2011 on the changing history of this area? After my marriage I moved to Easington Village in 1963 where my husband's family had lived for generations. As our three children grew up I became involved in village life, the Save the Children Club and Easington Community Association where John and I ran a Youth Club in the church hall for ten years.

When Easington Village Residents Association was formed I became Secretary and helped organise the Village Fair for 16 years raising money to improve the village. In 1983 Easington Village Parish Council was formed and I served as a councillor, serving as Chairman from 1991 – 2011. The new parish council was based at Seaton Holme which was used as a community venue, offices and a visitor centre.

I was always interested in local history and I researched the village history for the exhibition in Seaton Holme Discovery Centre and ran a self help group for Family History for many years. I didn't want this knowledge to be lost and the Parish Council funded my first book and with the help of local people who willingly shared their memories and photographs, *Easington – The Way We Were* was printed. The response to this was wonderful and I received letters from all over the world from ex-pats reminding them of their youth.

I ended my last book with a photo of Easington Colliery in the throes of destruction and I captioned it 'One day children will ask "What was a pit?" That day has come and in this book I would like to catch up on the lives of those people who will one day be part of this history.

Eileen Hopper
Easington, 2011

An aerial photo of Easington Colliery taken just before 1939. (Sunderland Echo)

OLD EASINGTON

Easington, what does the name entail? Talk to a stranger who doesn't know the area and one of the first recollections is the pit disaster in 1951 or the Miners' Strike in 1984. They never realise the long and ancient history of rural Easington stretching to the first documentation of the 900's when the lands of Easington were granted to Ealfrid by the Bishop. The discovery in 1991 of a pagan Anglo-Saxon burial ground proved earlier occupation of the area and was thought to be part of a much larger 6th or 7th century cemetery.

Easington, an episcopal manor, gave its name to one of the four wards of the Palatinate of Durham and was a very important place in days gone by; a large parish with the church overlooking the spacious village green. Historical records states: "The village of Easington, which gives its name to the ward and deanery, is situated on the turnpike road between Stockton and Sunderland on elevated ground, which gradually slopes towards the sea, and its church tower affords a good landmark to sailors."

Old Low Row.

On the eastern coast of Durham, it lies on a magnesian limestone plateau with boulder clay above and it is rare for such outcrops to exist near the sea. Laid down during the Permian period, 240 million years ago, it is formed from the remains of the skeletal structures and shells of countless animals.

The church of St Mary the Virgin.

County Durham is unique, as for many centuries it was a virtually independent state ruled not by the king, but by powerful 'Prince Bishops', who were more or less the 'Kings of County Durham'. The Domesday Book of 1086, the earliest surviving public record of the lands held by William the Conqueror and his people did not include Durham. The Boldon Book compiled in 1183 gave a detailed account of the rents and dues owed to the Bishop of Durham by the tenants under his control either produce, labour or service at special times of the year. Almost 200 years later Bishop Hatfield's survey was compiled from 1377 with services due to the Bishop of Durham from his tenants and their lands. The Bishops governed the County with both military and financial independence; they frequently had to repel Scottish invasions, by their own forces and at their own expense, until Henry II brought Durham into main government rule.

Between these surveys the life of the residents had changed dramatically with the invasion of the Scots in the 13th century who ravaged the land down to the Tees. Then in 1349 the plague, the Black Death, struck as it journeyed across the length and breadth of Britain and it was thought to have reduced the population of Durham by one third. The 15th century was a time of poverty, misery, oppression and war affecting residents both high and low decimating the population.

In 1569 there was the 'Rising of the North' intended to remove the Protestant Elizabeth Tudor from the throne and replace her with the Catholicism and in retaliation two men were reputed to be hanged on the village green. The Civil War of 1642, with the beheading of King Charles I and the rule of Oliver Cromwell also had an affect on Easington when the local men signed the Solemn League and Covenant. In 1664 it is noted the Scottish Army is on Easington Hill (could that be Andrew's Hill?). Before the Enclosure Decree Awards of 1656-72, Easington was surrounded by moors and closes; many of their names are carried on by today's farms.

Rosemary Lane.

Church floodlit (Keith Craig).

EASINGTON – THE CHANGES

Easington was a thriving rural village with mills and farms both in and around the village. Well served with numerous shops, tailors, bootmakers and butchers, and public houses serving the neighbouring countryside. The stage coaches stopped there daily bringing passengers and mail. The layout of four rows of houses round the green is medieval, with its pond and grazing for animals. It was also the site of fairs and social events over the centuries.

In 1870 it was described thus: "EASINGTON, a village, a township, a parish, a sub-district, a district, and a ward in Durham. The village stands 2 miles from the coast, 2 E of Haswell railway station, and 9 E by N of Durham; it occupies an elevated site and was anciently a place of importance."

Seaside Lane was a narrow rural lane leading to the coast passing the Workhouse built in 1850. Low Row was faced by Front Street; where now new houses stand. Clappersgate was an ancient street mentioned in records of 1602 and behind Rosemary Lane there were streets with humble cottages and lodging houses.

Villagers collected their water from street pumps until they were found to be unfit for human consumption, spreading typhoid, and in 1895 they were filled in and street taps provided.

Clappersgate Half Moon.

The Village Green was dissected by roads leading to major towns until replaced by footpaths as part of the restoration work. The old milestone still stands on the Green.

A rare and exciting find in 1991 of a badly disturbed Anglo-Saxon cemetery with 26 graves, by a man using a metal detector, at Andrew's Hill proved earlier habitation of the area. Fragments of bronze, dress jewellery worn by Anglo-Saxons during the 6th century were found. A 4th century copper alloy buckle was earlier found close to Thorpe Beck – the only direct evidence for Roman period activity.

Easington Poor Law Union started in 1837 overseen by an elected Board of 22 Guardians representing the 19 parishes that eventually became Easington District Council. In 1903 the offices for the Board of Guardian of the Poor were constructed in Seaside Lane; it also housed the Easington Rural District Council. The original part of the building still stands with numerous additions; it also housed the area's Registry Office before it moved to Peterlee. It finally closed its doors as the District of Easington council on 31st March 2009 when Durham County Council became the unitary authority and the offices moved to Spectrum Park in Seaham.

Independent representative's flyer for election in 1983.

Over the years the old houses were knocked down leaving spaces and waste land for many years; Rosemary Lane was waste ground until the council built new houses. The Council Yard moved to Peterlee and the Spinney estate was built. Around the Green, once surrounded by houses, Southside and Low Row remained and the spaces where the old houses had been replaced by modern houses.

Easington Village was designated as a Conservation Area in 1974 in recognition of its history. The Village Green was dissected by roads with the old A19 crossing it with the old milestone. The present A19 was built; the Green roads closed in 1977 and were replaced with footpaths and tidied up, overhead wires were put underground, the church floodlit in 1979 and the old mud tracks of Low Row replaced with scoria blocks with responsibility to go to Easington District Council.

Originally the parish council was known as Easington covering both the colliery and village but when Easington Village Residents Association was formed, and boundary changes allowed, a questionnaire showed

Thresher at West View.

the majority of village residents wanted their own parish. This was formed in 1983 and the two parishes split into Easington Colliery Parish Council and Easington Village Parish Council. This new council had to start completely from scratch. They built a cemetery lodge and purchased Seaton Holme as a community building for local groups to meet and headquarters for themselves and Groundwork East Durham.

Right: Brampton House. In 1929 it was the Brampton House Social Club & Institute and it can be remembered by older folk as the Food Office during the Second World War. In this photograph it looks like a private house.

Left: Holly House and Church Walk. Bunting makes us think it is the time of Queen Victoria's Diamond Jubilee.

Rosemary Lane with the original houses and Lion House, the shop was then owned by W. W. Carr. It was pulled down when the new houses were built and the lion above the door was taken to Sunderland.

The original swing park as it was known was for many years behind North Crescent. This secluded area was deemed not suitable due to anti-social behaviour and after consultation with experts the Village Green was chosen. The parish council had to fight the district council to put it there in 1990 as it seemed a safer place for children to play. The wooden structures became worn out and money was raised over the years for their replacement.

The new swings, built in 2008, faced by the new houses that replaced old ones from years ago.

St Mary's Brownies and Guides celebrate Queen Elizabeth II Coronation in 1953 with a Maypole display on the Village Green.

Braehead situated at the top of the Green, next to the Church, was built on the site of two cottages. The white house next door was the Church Reading Rooms and Billiard Room at one time. The Form Seat, in front of the church, has stood on the site longer than the date shown 1897, as it was repaired that year by the parish council. The cross of the Roman Catholic Church can be seen to the left and the car is numbered GR 2813.

Looking down the Green – the fronts look most unsightly and the top houses have now been modernised. Low Row was a muddy track running in front of the houses until Easington District Council started a scheme in 1979 to make the conservation area more attractive.

Pubs have closed and the Kings Head once an old coaching inn and a centre for meetings is now being turned into flats and more built in the old yard. The many changes that have taken place over the years can be seen in these photos.

Removing one of the last old red phone boxes in Thorpe Road.

This once in a lifetime view takes a while to work out – taken from upstairs in Seaside Lane by Bill Day, it shows the new flats, the King's Head before the roof was replaced, the bottom of Rosemary Lane and the church tower at the top of the hill.

The Kings Head, built pre 1828, was a coaching inn, the oldest inn in Easington. After it closed it stood like this deteriorating while waiting to be renovated as flats. Work started at the end of 2010 and is still ongoing.

The Half Moon much altered from the original old building.

EASINGTON COLLIERY

In 1899, near the coast, the Easington Coal Co began sinking the first of three shafts; much delayed by water encountered in the 500 feet of limestone which overlies the coal seams. The sinking of the North Pit was finished in September 1901 but the first coal was not brought out until 1910.

Wooden sinkers' huts were the first buildings in Easington Colliery followed by rows of streets to house the miners coming from all parts of Britain. They needed shops, pubs, cinemas and schools and the colliery became bigger than the village and Seaside Lane became the main shopping area. There were three Co-ops, selling all sorts of clothing and three cinemas, with their thrice weekly programmes.

Once a busy, thriving centre providing everything needed, the Co-ops were taken over and once the pit went many more shops closed and families moved away. Streets were pulled down and, like many places, out of town shopping complexes have dealt the final blow to the small shop keepers.

Easington Colliery Water Works with staff houses.

Seaside Lane from Bede Street junction showing all the well used shops, circa 1930s.

Looking up Seaside Lane towards the Easington Colliery Infant and Junior School. When the pupils moved to their new school it had a Grade II listed building category put on the former Girls and Boys blocks, manual instruction block, bicycle sheds and walls, piers, gates and railings. The school was built in 1911-13 by J. Morson of Durham and classrooms had wood and glass screens to corridors, and wooden parquet floors.

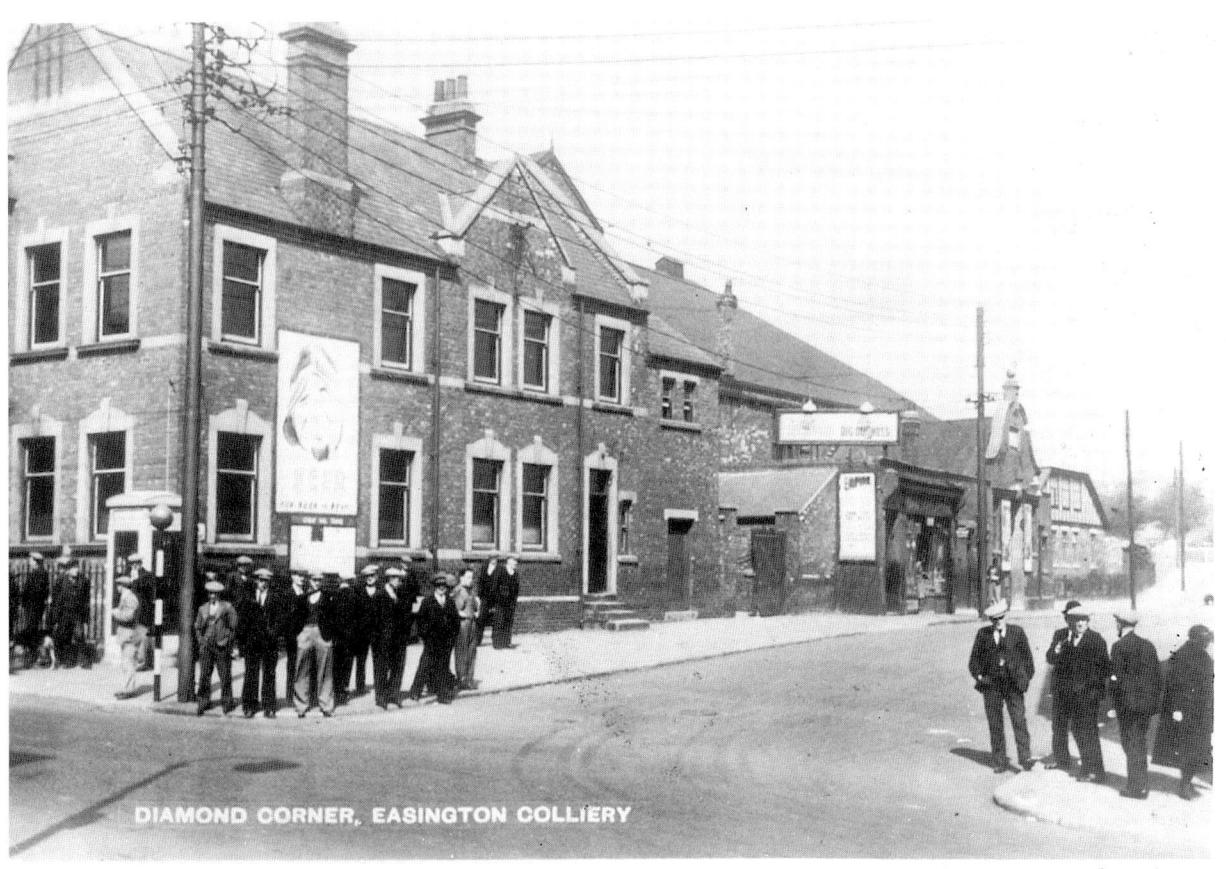

The corner of the Black Diamond with the Empire cinema behind; this is now the site of the doctor's surgery. The Diamond, like lots of modern pubs, has changed its name to something trendy – The Derby – but is still struggling to survive.

Above: The colliery with the pit head baths and the A streets.

The miner's life was hard graft – descending into the bowels of the earth by cage after changing into work clothes; collecting their lamps and identity tokens, before travelling along the underground roadways to their place of work. They worked in shifts hewing the coal, loading the trucks or shoring up the walls bringing up the Black Diamonds that were their livelihood.

Above: An unusual view of the pit wheel when it was lowered for repairs. The men show how large it was.

Left: Demolition of Ayre and Abbott Streets as local people moved out of the area after the closing of the pit.

Group of colliery men.

Jack Dormand MP and John Crockett Shift Manager.

The view along the sidings – 1300 feet pit bottom level.

The Shearer face in the High Main Seam.

Stan Turner and Bill Beadnell.

40 HP Endless Haulage machine

Typical sea coal carriers with sacks on their bike.

In 1926 the General Strike began when the owners intended to reduce the miners' wages and to lengthen their hours. During the strike the men were not eligible for unemployment benefit. The Canteen Committee supervised the serving and preparation of meals and teachers, churches and chapels all did their bit. Volunteers worked at large outdoor boilers to cook the food and serve it to the needy. It dragged on through the months until hardship forced men to begin to drift back to the mines. Their lives changed eventually for the better; in 1927 the first pit head baths opened and in 1938 the first holidays with pay and the mines were nationalised in 1947.

Here are three views of work at local soup kitchens in 1926. In the top photograph it looks like the school in the background and Haswell Store cart.

People have turned out to see these ponies as they spent most of their life underground. Pit ponies were stabled underground and were used to pull tubs of coal out of the coal seams. In 1913, there were 70,000 ponies underground in Britain, by 1984, there were 55. Tony, who was thought to be the last pit pony living, died July 2011 in an animal shelter.

Working men's clubs were popular but over the years many have closed but the Easington Colliery Club & Institute is still going strong with its annual leek shows, pigeon events and entertainment. Easington Colliery Working Men's Club opened in 1912 (*photograph above*) and a new lounge costing £5,000 was built in 1963 for the 1,200 members. In 1964 fire swept through the building blowing off the roof and it was gutted in 90 minutes. The present club was then built and is still popular especially at weekends with its entertainment programme. Most other clubs in the area closed.

A night at the club in 1958 for Terry, John, Tot, Alan and Bernie.

DURHAM BIG MEETING
(The Gala)

The Big Meeting or Miners' Gala started in 1871 in Wharton Park, Durham moving to the Racecourse Ground in 1939. Everyone made their way to the Gala by bus or train. Banners from all the pits were carried, draped with black after a death at the pit, followed by the bands and crowds marching through the city centre. The flags and banners were a rallying point for union members proclaiming their past achievements.

Above: Two little mini-bandsmen mascots stand proudly with Easington Colliery Band conductor Bill Gelson in 1950 at the Durham Gala. People from each colliery were proud to march behind their lodge banner.

Left: Standing with the banners at Durham are Alan Cummings & Billy Stobbs, union men, also B. Corner, J. Forster, D. Storey, T. Sharp and A. Pitt.

Above: Gathering at the corner of Seaside Lane, showing the pit in the background, with the banner ready to march.

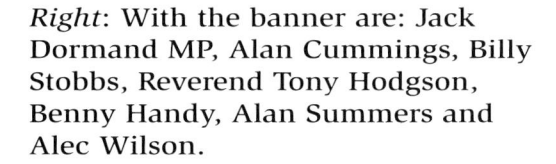

Right: With the banner are: Jack Dormand MP, Alan Cummings, Billy Stobbs, Reverend Tony Hodgson, Benny Handy, Alan Summers and Alec Wilson.

Outside Durham Cathedral for the special miners' service.

The Garside and Ord families with friends enjoying the Big Meeting in 1985 outside the Labour Party tent.

THE EASINGTON MINING DISASTER, 1951

On 29th May 1951 an explosion occurred at Easington Colliery and 81 miners lost their lives and two rescuers brought the final death toll to 83. The explosion occurred around 4.30 am in an area known as the 'Duck Bill' as the coal dust exploded bringing down the roof and causing rock falls. It couldn't have happened at a worse time as it was between shifts with 43 men of the fore shift about to take over from the 38 stone shift men who had worked overnight. Most, if not all, families had someone or knew someone who worked at the pit. A disaster fund was set up and, within 12 hours, £3,600 had been raised, reaching a total of £180,000 – a massive amount for those days. An Avenue of Trees was planted at the Welfare Park with a single tree for each man who died in the tragedy and a tablet placed on a stone from the scene of the accident to honour the memory of those who lost their lives.

Friends and relatives gather outside the colliery houses following the disaster.

Stricken Village is told there is no hope for miners
Women Break Down as News is Given

Easington Colliery is today a village without hope. In little colliery houses in almost every street women are mourning the loss of some relation, killed 900 feet below ground in the Five Quarter Seam. Late last night the crowds at the colliery gates made way for miners' leader Sam Watson, who walked bare-headed among the miners and their wives, climbed up the steps of a colliery house and turned to tell them: "There is no hope." As a weary team of rescue workers, with oxygen masks and rescue apparatus hanging from their shoulders trudged wearily from the pit cage to the rest room he told the crowd how these courageous squads had been battling for 40 hours to find the entombed men.

Sunderland Echo, 31st May 1951

Right: The funeral is shown of the 72 miners in Easington Colliery cemetery. All the graves are together in the garden area laid out side by side and memorials built where the victims are buried. Special graveside services were held to mark each decade and miner's lamps unveiled each time. A cutter from the pit stands near the graves. Family members and descendants travel from all over to show their respects.

Easington Colliery Pit Disaster 60th Anniversary 2011

The disaster is still commemorated with families coming to remember their loved ones. In 2011 a display was organised by the local community and schoolchildren with help from Beamish Museum. Displayed in the Welfare Hall was a commemorative banner of 60 panels each designed and painted by a members of the community. There was also paintings, glass and art work, with drama created by local school pupils and memorabilia from local residents. On the anniversary day a parade marched from the Memorial Garden on the old pit site to the Church of the Ascension for a service, then to the graves in the cemetery.

There are three widows still alive: Jenny Blevins 86, Eva Hunt 99 and Margaret Lippeatt 93. At the service Margaret's daughter Shirley, who was five when her father died and couldn't understand what had happened to him, read a poem written this year by her mother:

Margaret Lippeatt with husband Joe and son Joe.

An Epilogue to my husband Joe

My name is Margaret Lippeatt this year I will be 93,
My thoughts often go back to how it used to be.
I had a loving husband, two wonderful children
I was proud of my family.
Until that awful day in May when all happiness was taken away,
I was confused and lost but had to be strong
I could not be brave, everything was wrong.
The children were too young to understand
But people were kind and held out a helping hand.
Sixty years have passed since you were taken away
But the ache in my heart, dear Joe, is still with me today.
The children have grown up and have families too
I know in my heart you have helped me through.
I am left with fond memories that will never fade away
And with God's help I will stay strong and face another day.

Jenny Blevins had a daughter Carol and was four months pregnant with her son, Alan when she heard the dreadful news. A month later she wrote this verse that is now framed in her son's home in Canada.

The Price of Coal

The price of coal as far as we
The wives and mothers of miners see
Is far too dear as I will tell
Of that day that made our lives a hell,

As they gathered round the pit head baths
They shared a joke and had some laughs
They took their lamp and took their bait
And went down the mine that sealed their fate,

Other men whose work was through
They'd mined more coal for me and you
Talked of home and bairns and wives
When the explosion took their lives.

Around the country news soon spread
And wives and friends all left their beds
With anxious face – tear filled eyes
Bravely trying to hide their sighs.

The hours wore on without good news
The local lads expressed their views
They'd got one up – no two – no three
We prayed in silence you and me,

Day after day the people waited
The news of loved ones so ill fated
Hearts full of sorrow, brave even when
The last hope went for those 81 men.

In a churchyard on a hill
There our men lie peaceful still
Memories shall linger
Though time will roll
Of the price the miner pays for coal.

Matthew Blevins married Jenny Trotter in Horden in 1945. They lived in Inchape Terrace. Matthew was killed in the 1951 explosion at Easington Colliery when an ignition was caused by sparks from cutter picks striking pyrites.

Jenny Blevins, 86, and Margaret Lippeatt, 92, in 2011 at the luncheon club, they never remarried. They were typical of those wives left alone who raised their families showing strength and humour over the years.

Despite the loss of all these men work had to carry on and in 1962 Easington was the first single pit to reach the million tons of saleable coals target and was thought to have a thriving future. In an NCB information booklet of 1975 there were five seams the High Main, Main, Low Main, Yard and Hutton stretching as far as Easington Village with reserves to about six miles offshore. It was the pit with the biggest saleable output in the Durham coalfield with a productivity figure well above the national average. In 1955 employment reached 3,014 but by 1964 employment had dropped by 300.

For a number of years mines were closing and in 1984 the miners' strike started in protest. It lasted for a year and brought with it much hardship. The wives, mothers and daughters of the miners played a very important role during the strike, fundraising as well as staffing the soup kitchens. There were violent scenes at pit gates and police in riot gear came from other areas to join local police. When the strike ended things were never the same again and the county built on coal changed. Within ten years of the strike the 12 pits in this area had all closed including Easington, mothballed in 1993 and rased to the ground in 1994.

The 1984 Strike picket break – Standing two photographers. Left: ? Barber, Phil Barker. Right: John Jones, Harry Farlow. Sitting: Joe Newman, Billy Milburn, Billy Marr, John Maxwell; and sitting on kerb Davy Robinson and Ronnie Clarkson.

The pits left a lasting legacy, turning the North Sea black, destroying the seabed with pit shale and sludge. At first the sea washed away small amounts but after 1945 with mechanisation the spoil washed back onto the beaches in some places up to 10 metres thick. A common site was men with bikes carrying sacks of small coal up the steep incline from the shore; used to bank up fires at night in the all-night grate at home.

Where once the mine stood is now grass land with the only reminder the three tier pit cage, used to take the miners into the depths of the earth, standing at the top of the hill. There are also vents marking were the coal shafts were and a geological timeline explains the history of the pit.

Right: In May 2002, on her Golden Jubilee tour, HRH Queen Elizabeth visited the old colliery site and the new memorial garden for those men who worked there from 1899 to 1993. The Queen was introduced to three former rescue workers who vividly remembered the day of the disaster, Arthur Bartholomew (84) George Otterwell (77) and David Patton (78).

SCHOOLS

The first school in Easington was in 1814 when the Rector erected two rooms for a parochial charity school. Easington Village C of E School was built and catered for all ages; 80 pupils paid 1d a week in 1828. When the colliery schools were built it became a Primary School. It was pulled down in 1967 and the present school was built which attracted more pupils.

Left: The old Easington Village C of E School in 1890 – Standard 5, when Elizabeth Robinson attended. Mr William Wiggham was noted on the census as Master of Elementary Education and lived in Rose Cottage, the old school house on the corner of The Garth.

Easington Village C of E Primary School, circa 1960s. In no order: Jeffrey Raine, Alan Dobson, Billy Bower, Dianne Hornsby, Anne Bower, Margaret Brass, Marjorie Leith, Dorothy Mason, Cathleen Lynch, Marion Coxon, Noreen Parkin, Roberta Anne Brown, Christine Elliott, Vera Park, Colin Wright and Christine Shipley.

Right: A group of pupils from the C of E School in the 1940s. The teacher is in the background – two boys seem to be wearing paper hats so think it was a party and ages would be mixed. Pupils shown are: David Hutchinson, Lucy Dryden, Iris Mitchell, Ivy Coxon, Ann Tate, Kenneth Harrison, Arthur Laver, Andrew Rowden, Dorothy Howard, Lorna Patterson and David Bycroft.

Left: A C of E football team, 1969 with Mr Rowell. Back row: Gary Thompson, Paul Neasham, Marco Rigali, Mark Davison, Ross Greenwell, David Harrison, Paul Smith, Peter Robson. Front row: unknown, Jeff Jones, David Smith, Philip Reed, Stuart Park and unknown.

Right: Mr Gibson's class, 1970. Back row: Carol Barker, Sonia Parkin, Lynn James, Janice Dobson, Lesley Reed, Elaine Kellett, Joanne Pearce, Tina Parkin. Third row: Julie Park, Ross Greenwell, Geoffrey Sennett, unknown, Keith Hopper, Amadeo Rigali, David Smith, Ian Mawhinney, David Harrison, Paula Mawhinney, Susan Anderson, Joan Baker. Second row: Sandra Weatherall, Kay Martin, Margaret Kirkbride, Janet Craig, Mr Gibson Headmaster, unknown, Gillian Reed, Julie Neasham, Katherine Burnhope. Front row: Geoffrey Siggens, Billy Brookes, Beverley Jones, Andrew Patterson and Philip Reed.

Easington Village C of E Primary, from Matt Baker's year – 1985/86. Back row: Matthew Styles, Martyn Lee, Craig Barton, Anthony Parkin, Nicholas Parker, John Delanoy, Paul Schofield. Second row from back: Billy Hunter, Sarah Robson, Julie Ann Lawson, Rance Routledge, Gareth Harrison, John Paul Bridges, Claire Dosh, Claire Maddison. Second row: Amy Butters, Claire Smith, Emma Taylor, Mr Rowell, Joanne Delanoy, Lorraine Lamb, Claire Colwell. Front row: Anthony Maddison, Nicholas Duncan, Winston Garside, Matthew Baker, Lee Barton.

A familiar sight – Mr Smith, with his old dog, crosses Anita Craig, Yvonne Bell and Julie Forster.

Easington Colliery used a temporary tin school that quickly became over crowded as more miners came to work at the pit. By 1913 a large council school was being built. Kelly's Directory for 1914 says "Easington Colliery School for boys, girls and infants when completed will have cost £21,000 for 1296 children; average attendance 320 boys, 310 girls and 325 infants.

Right: Easington Colliery Girls Junior School, Summer 1950, with Miss Thompson (school clerk) and Miss Wardell (Headmistress). Pupils are: Joan Dobson, Mary Maddison, Marjorie Stephenson, Maureen Hall, Mavis Enwright, Ann Harriman, Joy Robson, Mavis Willis, Lorna Harrison, Marie Burnham, Shirley Devine, Lillian Craig, Joan Hood, Ann Fairs, Doreen Rider, Sheila Lauder, Marie Shield, Ann Wright, Hilda Johnson, Sheila Hodgson, Norma Robin, Margaret Adamson, Avril Jones, Marjorie Lamb, Margaret Meggison, Betsy Staple, Alice Walker, Ilean Wilson, Marjorie Wylam, Joan Grey, Freda Sanderson.

Children from Easington Colliery Primary School celebrated the 80th Anniversary with a photo display. They also dressed and played games from that era and were presented with commemorative mugs.

Gladys Watson, 94, visits her old school Easington Colliery Primary where she taught as Miss Underwood. With her are: Daniel Patterson, Rachael Harle, Luke Whittington, Stacy Hornsby, Keighley Harriman and Martin Dunn. She returned to Easington after living with her sister in the south and was visited regularly by her old pupils. Gladys died in 2005 at the age of 102.

Easington Colliery Senior Boys and Girls School was built in Whickham Street and Seaside Lane in 1938, for both senior colliery and village children. It was later known as the Secondary Modern, leaving the original schools for primary age pupils.
It originally had separate buildings for both boys and girls with class rooms and the hall set around open quadrangles.

Easington Colliery Modern School from the playing fields.

In 1978 a new school was built in Stockton Road for seniors and both schools served as a split site school until September 1993 when everyone transferred to Easington Village. It is now known as Easington Community Science College with further alterations to the school completed in 2011.

Easington Community Science College was awarded the Green Eco School flag in 2008 for their work in the school grounds.

The school had two badges – the first one was based on the tale of the Easington Hare then changed to the Comprehesive badge. The old senior school was demolished in 1994 and the new Whickham Street Primary School built on part of the site was opened in 1998 and pupils transferred. The old primary school closed in 1998 and was given Grade II listed status. This was a controversial subject as it was vandalised and stands dilapidated in 2011 and any bids to demolish the structure are opposed.

Left: A re-union of old girls from Easington Modern School.

An Easington Modern class, 1949. The photo is from Ada McKee (centre in back row). Others, in no order are: Sarah Softly, Eleanour Semons, Gloria Scott, June Lanthorn, Mary McCabe, Sheila Wright, Mabel Harper, ? Meggison, Jean Bott, Elsie Eils, Gloria Scott, Joyce Merritt, Maureen Bainbridge, Mildred Johnson, Greta Burnip, Maureen Barton, Edith Taylor. Joyce Stoker and Margaret Robson.

An Easington Modern class, 1951. Back row: M. Houghton, D. Thornton, M. Green, J. Spoors, J. Hood, M. Shield, J. Robson, M. Frank, I. Bell. Third row: A. Fairly, A. Wright, B. Dryden, L. Craig, A. Harriman, V. Wharton, Valda Pipe, J. Norfolk, D. Riley, M. Willis. Second row: M. Thompson, M. Sculley, M. Garside, D. Crawford, P. Coats, F. Stainson, M. Maddison, N. Enwright, J. Ramsey, F. Smith. Front row: V. Rothery, N. Meggison, I. Spate, H. Radistock, S. Hodgeson, I. Wilson.

Easington Modern School football team with their trophies. Back row: Mr Suffield, Les Sheiles, Billy Elves, Ken Jones, Billy Laverick, Denny Brown, Wilf Dixon, ? Pattison, Mr A. Johnson. Front row: Derek Brown, ? Jolly, Alan Robinson, Gordon Glaister and Billy Allison.

Easington Modern School football team – Proud winners of the B & O Shield and finalists in the Horden Hospital Cup County in 1949. Some of the names in the back row are: Allan Barrass, Leslie Carr, Ronnie Greener, Gordon Bradley, Mr Hill, Billy Laverick, Terry Pattinson, Billy Elliott, Eddie Townsend. Front row: Mr Johnson, Billy Stobbs, Ray Knapper, Billy Dawson, Billy Gibson, Head master Mr Suffield.

Right: Modern School football team. Back row: Mr Suffield Headmaster, Wilkinson, A Duff, J Fletcher, J, Garside, A. Green, K. Jones, A. Elliott, Mr Johnson. Front row: S. Knapper, O. Watson, A. Richmond, A. Robinson, G. Glaister, R. Jobson.

Easington Modern School football team– Finalists of the Cochrane Cup & B & O Shield, 1949/50. Back row: unknown, Billy Hills, Peter Holmes, unknown, Wilf Dixon, Billy Laverick, Ron Jones, Ken Jones, Mr St Julian. Front row: Mr Arthur Johnson, Derek Brown, Eddie Townsend, Billy Stobbs, Harry Jolly, Denis Brown, Mr L. Suffield.

Easington Modern School cricket team, 1947. Back row: J. Young, G. Bradley, G. Clapham, D. Jones, R. Hepple. Front row: R. Knapper, R. Ball, R. Greener, E. Wilkinson, E. Shanks, N. Watson.

Left: Easington Modern School class around 1951. Among the girls are: Freda Golightly, Audrey Stubbs, Eva Horton, Jean Reed, Freda Harker, Sadie Evans, Alma Bell and Margaret Crooks.

Secondary Modern School class, 1950. Included are: Benny Handy, Bob Harker, Billy Allison, H. Longstaff, Les Shields, Eddy Wynn, Eric Pattison, John Fickling, Colin Bell, Billy Laverick, Denny Brown, Derek Brown, Tom Grey, Roxby, H. Jolly and Tom Jones.

Easington Modern School class, 1960. Included are, back row: Aileen Reed, Ann, Jean Owen, Joan Smith, Teresa. Middle row: Carol Reed, Ann Tate, Brenda, Carol, Ann Stephenson, Claris Gates, Ann Pickard, Mary Bowman, Joyce Fairley, Winifred Johnson, Vivian Reed. Front row: Carol Ann Robinson, Olive Parkin, Marie Schofield, Jenny Warton, Audrey Welsh, Mrs Bradley, Jennifer Stratford, Marjorie Pickford, Phyliss.

The previous page shows two girls' classes and one boys' class. The girls are all looking very smart in their uniform but the class below is a mixed class and everyone is not wearing uniform, especially the boys.

Modern School class in 1961. Mr Reed is the teacher and among the pupils are: Richard Burnip, Barbara Vickers, Harry Turnbull, Robert Wilson, Thelma Williams, Peter Watson, Jack Taylor, Kenneth Delanoy, Alan Bower, John Turner, Ed Brown and Russell Shields.

Easington Modern School class around 1970. Unfortunately, not all names are know. Included back row: Edwin Little, Paul Hewitson, Kevin Wood, David Tate, Barry Jones. Middle row: Julie Colwill, Brendan Fox, John Defty, Hughie Hutton, Martin Turner, David Potts, Steven Milburn. Front row: Vicky Lee, Jean Stoker, Jeanette Burn, Mary Bruce, Mr Holden, Dianne Miller, Carol Quinn, Karen Davey, Gail Robson.

SPORT

The Welfare Park was the ideal place for sport. After spending hours in the darkness of the pit miners relished outdoor pursuits of football, cricket and bowls. Easington Colliery Welfare has always had its cricket teams and Matthew Oswald awarded a cup.

Easington Colliery AFC formed in 1913 as Easington Colliery Welfare came to fame in the 1930s in the Wearside League, winning five Championships and five Cup Finals. In 1955 Easington's biggest day came when a crowd of 4,500 saw the Colliery lose 2-0 to Tranmere Rovers in the first round of the FA Cup – the only time that Easington have reached the first round proper.

In 1980 the Welfare amalgamated with the highly successful Easington Rangers and Easington Colliery AFC was born. They moved up to the First Division and reached the final of the League Cup losing in the final to Spennymoor in extra time. In 2010 after a long spell without silverware the club lifted the Wearside League Cup with victory over Marske.

Football photos from all ages have been a popular donation and Easington had numerous clubs both when at school and in later life for adult sportsmen.

Swimming was popular in the early days before the aerial flight tipped coal waste into the sea. From 1948 over 500 youngsters joined the Swimming Club that used the colliery reservoir, after hard work to clean what was known as the 'pit pond'.

Trophies won by Easington Welfare 1931-32 – Wearside League Champions, National Orphanage Cup, Durham Memorial Cup.

Left: Old Scholars, 1949-50. Back row: Derrick Allen, Walter Hudspith, Keith Craig, Ralph Elvin, Paul Robinson, Jacky Powell. Front row: Tommy Barker, Ray Brown, Ronnie Bradley, ? Thompson, ? Lowry.

The final year at Easington Modern School before moving onto senior football. Back row: Billy Stobbs, Terence Pattinson, Billy Laverick, Ronnie Green, Billy Elliott, Leslie Carr, Eddie Townsend. Front row: Gordon Bradley, Ray Knapper, Billy Barass, Billy Dawson and Billy Gibson.

Easington Colliery Works Club, 1963. Back row: W. Metcalfe, Bob Barker, Alan Summers, Les Carr, M. Laverick, M. Alderson, Micky Solan, Billy Stobbs, Fred Price, Alan Featonby, Mr Parkin. Front row: H. Appleby, J. Garside, Derek Brown, Deny Brown and Terry McClusky.

Possibly the Central Club in August 1967. Back row: Smith, Ingram, Richard Breward, ?, Dave Thomley, Ed Brown. Front row: ?, Reuben Watson, Harold Appleby, Maxy McClurey and Freddie Price.

Easington Colliery Works Club, 1962. Back row: Maurice Alderson, Martin Laverick, Les Carr, Billy Laverick, Billy Stobbs, Maxy McClurey, Mr Parkin (Trainer). Front row: Harold Appleby, Freddie Price, Derek Brown, Dennis Brown and John Garside.

Right: Looks like the Welfare ground. Included are back row: Les Ingram, Alan Summers, Archer, Cliff Price, Fred Price, Bobby Barker. Front row: D. Lyons, B. McNaney, Ted Handy, B. Handy, Maxy McClurey, and W. Metcalfe.

Left: A team in front of the old Welfare Park Pavilion sometime in the 1920s. I like the little boy holding the ball.

Right: Easington Colliery Welfare Bowls Club was founded in 1923 and in 1957 were the first champions of the newly formed Welfare Veterans' Coast Bowls League. They have had successful years as either winners or runners-up in the league and have had many successful father and son players. Not to be outdone the ladies decided to form their own team in the early 1980s and joined the Hartlepool District League. The pavilion was used to store equipment and provide teas.

PASTIMES

The Scout and Guides worked with the young people in both villages from the 1920s with flourishing groups as well as the Boys' Brigade and Methodist groups joining in with other local groups for competitions and camping.

Back in 1926, Easington Village was introduced to Guiding by Priscilla Allanson and a troop of Brownies was also started with Gwen Routh as the first Brown Owl. Over the years many people gave their time and expertise to Guiding, passing their work over to a younger generation as time went by. They have celebrated numerous anniversaries and events inviting the older generations of Guides to join in.

Right: The First Guides. Back row: Miss Cracknell, F. Harwood, R. White, E. Rowcroft, P. Toll, L. Cracknell, P. Fairs, Miss Duff. Front row: Halcrow, P. Toll, M. Charlton, E. Holmes, S. Cruddace, F. Allison, V. Chapman, R. Allison, A. Duff and M.A. Ramsay.

Seaham Division Brownies, 1954. They are not all Easington girls but those identified are: Ivy Green, Diane Trainer, Dorothy Smith, Dorothy Green, Mary Armstrong, Jean Laver, Doreen Rowden, Sheila Davison, Christine Lawson, Elaine Wylam, Rena Phillips, Christine Phillips, and Susan Davison.

Right: 1st Easington Guides win the Camping Cup, Seaham Division, 1972. Back row: Karen Mawhinney, Sandra Wiseman, Verna and Janice Kaye, Janet Smith, Sandra Dickinson, Susan Watson. Front row: Heather Lawson, Paula Mawhinney, Jill Dickinson and Susan Jones. The Guide Captain was Dorothy Green.

Left: 1st Easington Guides (Church) celebrate the 75th Anniversary of the Girl Guide movement – 1910-1985. Back row: Jeanette and Jacquiline Haw, Emma Hopper, Anna, Beverly Miller, Gillian Storey, Judy, Catherine Storey, Tracy Park. Middle row: Amber Cairns, Kathryn, Catherine Maley, Christine, Hilary. Front row: Susan Hopper, Helen Carter, Nicola Coils, Nicola, Sarah, Melanie and Andrea.

Right: 1st Easington Guides with the Camping Cup & Shield in the Division Competitions, May 1979. Back row: Lisa Forster, Julie Stephenson, Nora Vaughn. Front row: Julie Forster, Joanne Monaghan, Stephanie Parker, Joanne Irving and Sharon Moor.

Left: The County Commissioner for South Durham presents Sarah MacPherson, 10, with the North East of England Girl Guide award for tremendous courage. Sarah had spina bifida and was confined to a wheelchair but joined in with events.

Right: Thanks to Easington Amateur Radio Society, Easington Brownies dressed in uniforms from many lands and spoke to other Brownies far away by radio as part of Thinking Day in 1992. Gemma Carr, Eileen Robson, Helen Adamson, Emma Shilling, Ashley Iveson, Deborah Millburn and Julie Lowther watch Lisa Robinson on the airways with Alan Brown.

Left: To mark the 100th Anniversary of Guiding in 2010 Brownies and Guides planted a flower bed on the Village Green with the Easington Village in Bloom committee.

Bessie and Nollie Dryden at Moor House Farm, Durham Road.

The four boys are, left to right: John Chisholm, Alan Milburn, Robert Prest and Redvers Garside.

Left: Rovers Juniors, 1948. They are from Moncrieff Terrace and West Avenue. Back row: Alan Green, Derek Robinson, Eddie Lawson, Ian Harriman, John Garside. Centre: Billy Jameson. Front row: Harold Appleby, Ronnie Merritt, Harry Penick; right in front Peter Green.

Children enjoy the festivities at the WI Christmas party in the church hall in 1955. Included are: Doreen Rowden, Sheila Davison, Christine Lawson, Elaine Wylam, Rena Phillips, Christine Phillips, and Susan Davison.

Over the years youngsters could go to youth clubs, be coached in many sporting events, trained by the Colliery Band or just follow their many interests.

The St John Ambulance Brigade, who provided backing for medical emergencies, also trained the youngsters as cadets and many went on to nursing careers.

Kushiro Karate Club has been established since 1973 and now holds their classes in St Mary's Church Hall. The club has members of the England Karate Team within its ranks; two of whom are members of the European and World Championship winning England Team.

As with many colliery areas, two local brass bands started in 1915 supported by the miners and good players were encouraged to move from other areas of Durham to Easington. Two players were killed in the disaster of 1951 and the band led all the processions and played at the funerals of the victims. The two bands amalgamated in 1956 and in 1995 celebrated their 80th Anniversary with an exhibition in Seaton Holme and a concert in St Mary's Church. The band still took part in competitions across the country, but after losing its main sponsor was facing a bleak future. They bought new premises for training and a grant from the National Lottery of £45,000 in 1995 helped buy new instruments as theirs were on loan. In 2008 the Channel Four programme *The Secret Millionaire* saw marketing millionaire Carl Hopkins, who came incognito, help the community with a generous donation. He saw the importance of the band to Easington and links to its mining past and wanted to help them survive and presented them with a £10,000 cheque. With that and the publicity from the programme the band has gone from strength to strength and he is now the Lifetime Honorary President of the band

The band encourages youngsters to take up music and instruments are available for practice and they enjoy playing in the band.

Easington Colliery Band took part in the annual march at Tolpuddle in 2008. Trade Unionism in England had its beginnings with the Tolpuddle Martyrs.

THE CHURCHES

The church of St Mary the Virgin is a Grade 1 listed building founded in 1197. Built on the site of an earlier church, it can seen for miles around and Rectors of Easington until 1832 were also Archdeacons of Durham. It celebrated its 800th Anniversary with installation of new church bells and the restoration of the 150 year old organ.

The first rectory is now known as Seaton Holme, opposite the church in Hall Walks, followed in 1921 by the second further up Hall Walks and is now in Tudor Grange.

An old photograph of St Mary's Church and the Church of Our Lady of Victories and St Thomas, they never seemed so close together in later years as they were surrounded by trees. Roman Catholics built the Church of Our Ladies of Victories and St. Thomas in 1875 with the last mass in 1976; it is now the site of St. Thomas Close. The colliery was served by the Church of Our Lady of Assumption from 1923 until 1978 when both churches were pulled down and the Church of our Lady built in Cemetery Road.

Above: The old St Mary's church hall ready for a dance. The old church hall served the community well; it was erected in 1920 from two army huts from World War I. While it was still in use Easington Village Residents Association raised funds to provide a garden and car park on the surrounding land but this had to be removed when the new community hall was built with a Heritage Lottery Grant in 2000. This is used for local events, youth and sporting groups.

The old St Mary's parish hall was used for weddings, dances and youth groups and had a library and billiard room.

Left: The Eco-Congregation Award was presented by TV botanist and wildlife guru and naturalist David Bellamy in February 2003. Under the leadership of the late Myra Stonley, St Mary's was the first church in the Durham Diocese to reach Eco-Congregation status for its volunteer work around the churchyard with its magnesium limestone meadow. Part of this has been left uncut to show the natural flora.

THE CHURCH OF THE ASCENSION – The Mission Church was consecrated in 1913 then the new church named the Church of the Ascension was opened on Ascension Day 1929. The first church hall was replaced in 1974 by the present church hall. Many people remember the Church Centre used by all ages for sport and entertainment.

Above: The original Easington Colliery C of E church.

Above: Serving the teas at the Ascension Church Fair. From left: June Winter, Vena Burnham, and holding teapot is Olive Emerson.

Left: Churchwarden Mildred Bridges with Bishop Tom when he visited the Church of the Ascension.

Michael Solan and Doreen Thornton met at 14 while they were sledging and married in Our Ladies of Victories and St Thomas 1950.

Alan Robson and Ada McKee from Easington Colliery celebrated their Golden Wedding in 2007.

Eleanour Edgoose and Maurice Wake married at St Mary's and celebrated their Diamond Wedding in 2010.

Allan Clough from Littlethorpe married Doris Smith in 1954 in the Church of the Ascension.

Jack Hopper married Kitty Dryden in St Mary's in August 1931.

The Methodist Chapel in Easington opened in Low Row in 1885 and Easington Colliery started their first Methodist services in people's homes. The first chapel opened in Easington Colliery in 1910 and the three Colliery chapels united in 1959.

Children stand with the bounty of the Harvest Festival at Easington Village Methodist Church in Low Row.

Ladies in waiting helping at a wedding in St Mary's Hall in the 1950s. Left to right: Amy Horton, Mrs Broad, Peggy Willis, Mrs Stonehouse, Mrs Allen, Mrs Hillary, Annie Walton and Minnie Green.

WORK AND FAMILIES

As well as the many farmers and millers in the area the village had its own blacksmiths, at one time there were three smithies, who also repaired carts and wagons as well as shoeing horses. The Hornsby family were in Easington in 1841 and their smithy was in Stockton Road situated next to Delanoy's undertakers. The last blacksmith was Tommy who died in 1970 and some of the descendants of William Hornsby, who had nine children, are shown below.

Two of William Hornsby's daughters Nora & Jennie.

Tom Hornsby, blacksmith with a horse.

Nora's children, the twins are Ivy and Ivor Henderson, 1927

Jennie and her son Willie.

Left: The Thompson family, shown with horses, were contractors and carriers. I don't know where this is but the sign says 'Flats for Sale'.

This photograph looks like a coal delivery; note the shovel and the hatch that led from the backlane into the coal house where sacks of coal could be tipped. The sign on the cart says 'A. Thompson – Contractor. Easington Colliery'.

Right: The Thompson family descendants enjoy a day at Crimdon Beach in 1939. Crimdon was a popular holiday area for surrounding towns and villages and they travelled there on the buses to enjoy time on possibly the only golden sands in the area.

Right: Collins shop at Grants Houses – Lucy Dinning and Jenny Collins. It must be before decimalisation in 1971 as note the pricing 1s/5d. The Collins family moved to Rosneath, Grants Houses in 1967. Jenny worked in the shop while George Collins used to sell fresh fruit and vegetables in his transit van. They used to have three people working in the shop on Saturdays as they were so busy and the queue used to go right up the street. In those days, before supermarkets, Easington shops always had lots of customers. The Collins bought the Edgoose farm at Paradise Crescent now called Market Garden Farm where daughter Claire still lives. The family eventually went into a taxi and minibus business.

Left: A crowd of business people and their families from the Easington area enjoying a day trip.

Right: Staff at the Easington branch of Murton Co-operative Store in the 1930s. Names known are, back row, 2nd from left, Paddy Frain; 4th George Collins Horsekeeper; 5th Billy Gibson; 7th Bobby Robinson. Centre of the picture is Mr Ferguson the Manager.

Many people worked in the Board Offices for the Easington Rural Council or the Education and Youth Employment Office in Holly House, now converted into private houses and Kittie's shop next door became garages.

Easington Divisional Education Department was situated at Holly House. Jean Davidson is presented with a handbag by Mr J.H. Veitch before leaving for Canada in May 1957.

In the garden of Holly House are: Mark Yellow, George Gardner, Jean Davidson, Henry Gorton, Pat Palmer, June Todd, Sanna Miller and Jean Edgar.

Right: Staff from Holly House visiting the Mason's Arms. Included are: Ernie Sanderson, June Todd, Jean Davidson, George Gardner, Sally Maddison, Jean Edgar and Ted McEwan.

THE ITALIAN INPUT – Alfredo Donnini came from Barga in Tuscany and arrived in this country in 1899. He settled with his wife Catherine Brown in Easington Colliery and had an ice cream shop in Seaside Lane. Other families came and opened shops in Easington and were well known over the generations. The known names were Donnini, Passerotti and Equi and these families intermarried and became part of the colliery history.

Above: Louis Donnini with the ice cream van.

Left: Three men of the family looking very dapper.

Right: Noted amongst the family was Dennis Donnini, 19. He was the youngest soldier to win the Victoria Cross in the Second World War. He served as a fusilier in the Royal Scots Fusiliers and in an attack was wounded in the head and, on recovering consciousness, with the survivors of his platoon, pursued the Germans. Under intense fire he carried wounded comrades. Though again wounded, he advanced firing a machine gun until a bullet hit a grenade that he was carrying and killed him. The old people's home is named in his memory.

Above: The marriage of Veronica Donnini and Celestino Passerotti in 1927. Best man Louis Donnini, groom Louis Maggore, bridesmaids include Sylvia and Corrina Donnini, Flora Fiore and Peggy Wells.

Right: The marriage of Sylvia Donnini and Donald Putsman, 1946.

Corrina Donnini married Mauro Ferri in 1953. Bridesmaids are nieces Ines Passerotti, Anita Egin and Catherine Putsman, grooms Ronnie Ronaldo and Stanley Equi followed by Alfie, Gladys and Teresa Donnini.

Ines Passerotti married John Turner in 1954 who came from Ardrishaig on Loch Fyne, Scotland. He came to Easington in 1953 to work at the RAF sub-station at Cold Hesleden. They had five children John, Lindsey, Martin, Fiona and Robert and 10 grandchildren. Ines and John with some of their family are shown right.

THE SECOND WORLD WAR

On the edge of Easington Tuthill Quarry was a place of employment for many local people over the years. A disused Magnesian Limestone quarry, it was opened in 1923 to make explosives for mining and quarrying until 1936 when it became part of ICI. In the 1939-45 war it became a Munitions Filling Factory with 1,000 people doing 'war work' in three shifts. There was a mineral railway line from Tuthill Quarry via the former Hawthorn Cokeworks to Ryhope. It closed in the 1960s and was eventually used to tip coal into and is now listed as a Site of Special Scientific Interest.

Apart from sending its men to war Easington also had their own Home Guard Unit and ARP group for volunteers who could not enlist. A quarter of a million men in the country volunteered for the Home Guard on the first day of recruitment – although it was months before they had uniforms or weapons.

Right: Home Guards, a volunteer formation of local men, no one can identify the background. Men who joined the Home Guard could not join the regular army because of their age or necessary jobs.

The most significant day in the Battle of Britain as far as the north-east is concerned was 15th August 1940. This was the day the German Luftwaffe attempted to saturate the British Defences with attacks on the east coast. They met heavy opposition and suffered serious casualties. A direct hit was made on an occupied house and a man killed while riding a horse. Easington Colliery had approximately fifty houses damaged, twelve people were killed, most of the deaths occurring in Station Road, thirty people were injured. Little Thorpe Hospital also suffered damage and ten people were injured, these were the first civilian casualties of the war in Easington.

"A remarkable family record in national service is that of Joseph and Elsie Green of Manor House who have 11 sons and one daughter. Eight sons are in uniform. William, 39, in the Australian Forces, Jack, 31, Royal Artillery, Jimmy, 29, a sergeant in Bomber Command, Andrew, 27, the Royal Navy, Alan, 24, a leading aircraftsman in the Middle East, George, 22, in the Pioneer Corps, Desmond, 18, in the Royal Navy and Maurice, 16, in the Air Training Corps. Three other sons – Charles is at Easington Colliery, Joseph, a limestone quarryman, and Fred, a farmer. Their daughter Lily Burdess works in an Ordnance factory and is married to a miner." From *Durham Chronicle* July 1943.

| Maurice | James | George | Andrew | Alan | Jack | Desmond | William |

WELFARE HALL

Easington Colliery Welfare Hall opened in 1934, funded with money directly from the miners' pay cheques, so when the pit closed raising money became a struggle. It hosts the largest and best sprung dance hall in County Durham and still serves the community. It has benefited from over £366,000 worth of funding in the recent years to save the building from closure including £210,000 from the Big Lottery Grant and has plans for a major redevelopment.

In 2008 Carl Hopkins, from TV's *Secret Millionaire*, was impressed with the building and the opportunities the committee of volunteers provided for youngsters and presented a cheque for £12,000 for the dance hall, stage lights, curtains and equipment for the drama club. He was guest of honour at their first Christmas pantomime 'Aladdin'.

Easington Colliery Social Welfare Centre secretary, Cyril Dunn, impressed Carl as the "driving force" behind the work on the Welfare Hall and played an important role in keeping it open and making it a better place for the community. He was a trustee at the centre, in Seaside Lane, before becoming secretary and spent the past 20 years helping to revive the 1934-built building. Sadly Cyril died aged 72 in June 2011.

Gilbert Ridley and his orchestra were favourites for those who loved to dance; he is shown at the Welfare Hall in 1944. The players were: Piano Leader Gilbert Ridley, Drums Dick Shepherd, Bass Barrie Baxendale, 1st Trumpet Tommy Reynolds, 2nd Trumpet Billy Dodds, 3rd Trumpet & Vocalist Jackie Barton, Trombone George Houghton, 1st Alto Sax & Clarinet Bob Thompson, 2nd Alto Sax & Clarinet Jack McManners, 1st Tenor Sax George Phillips and 2nd Tenor Sax Wilf Owens.

The inaugural meeting of Easington Ladies Welfare Club was in 1964 and attracted women of all ages. Dances were held each weekend; a popular place for surrounding villages. Trips away were also organised to places like Blackpool.

Ladies at the inaugural meeting of the Ladies Welfare Club. Included are: Mesdames Barker, Dorothy Lowe, Agnes Burnham, Laverick, Florrie Williams, Smith, Golightly, Peggy Philips, Leech, Hilda Deadman, Reed, Bannister, Metcalfe, Sparrows, Hilda Nicholson, Goodrum, Mary Sparrow holding Jim, Eva Garrett, Mary Bell holding Jimmy, Wharton, Welch, Ruth Pye, Wilson and Audrey Watson.

Cutting the cake at the Welfare Ladies birthday. Names not in order: Mesdames Sant, Vickers, Harker, Ellen Smith, Reid, Wilson, Florrie Collinson, Alice Stephenson, Audrey Watson, H. Nicholson, Welsh, Smith, Lamb and Gray.

HEALTH & ELDERLY

A new healthy living centre Healthworks officially opened its doors on 5th November 2007 based at the former Waterworks office building in Paradise Lane at a cost of over £750,000. Further extensions provided a drop-in point for local people to get medical care.

There were 12 public wells in the village and also wells in some homes, sanitation was bad with earth closets and open gutters. Infectious diseases were rife and the authorities ordered all public wells to be stopped up. Thorpe Waterworks pumped the water to street taps from the new reservoir at Andrews Hill, opened in 1895, and in the 1920s water was piped to houses.

A doctor's surgery opened in Arbroath House, Easington Colliery and the practice celebrated its 100th anniversary with a Fun Day at the new William Brown Centre in Peterlee and raised £915 for McMillan Cancer.

Apart from the miners' bungalows, special places were built for the aged. Donnini House was built for independent living as well as Rutherford House which celebrated its 21st birthday in 2009. Ashwood Nursing Home was built on part of the old secondary school site followed by Birchwood in 2002. Seaton Holme was a home for elderly men but was closed when Essyn House was built in the former walled garden in the 1960s. It was demolished in 2001 and in 2007 new houses called Essyn Court were built.

The Millennium Luncheon Club was started each Wednesday in Seaton Holme in May 2000 for those isolated by age and infirmity. Alan Miller was the Chairman and organised a group of volunteer chefs and helpers. Together they provided weekly lunches, special events and birthday celebrations and marked their 10th Anniversary with a special lunch, still with many of the original volunteers. They have also raised £6,500 for Great North Air Ambulance, Help the Heroes, Children in Need, Grace House Hospice, Haswell Mencap, Easington Village C of E Primary School and the Salvation Army.

Alan Miller presents a cheque for £1,154 to Brigadier Richard Felton for Help the Heroes, raised through various events, watched by some of the volunteers and members.

WORKHOUSE & HOSPITALS

The care of the poor was the responsibility of the church until 1834. Then the Poor Law came into force in 1837 and they needed somewhere to house the needy to cover the 19 parishes that eventually became Easington District Council. The Union Workhouse was built in 1850 on Seaside Lane. By the 1930s wards were being used as a hospital and it became Leeholme Hospital with seven wards and x-ray facilities, operations and outpatients appointments. Part of the old workhouse became wards for the elderly until its closure and it was demolished in 1971.

This part was used for hospital access with the main building in Seaside Lane replaced by council offices surrounded by grassed areas,

This photograph and the ones over the page show Christmas parties and members of staff at Leeholme but all of them cannot be identified. We have a list of names that held positions there. Matron Ms Hindmarsh, Matron's Assistant Greta Knight, Housekeeper Margaret Maitland, Cook Alice Stubbs, Porter Mr Punshon, Portress Mrs Punshon, Cleaners Jenny and Connie Craggs, Nurses Betty Collins and Betty Smith, General Assistant Mavis Franklin, Chambermaid Jenny Usher and Boilerman Ernie Collins.

Staff at Leeholme enjoy a Christmas party in the hospital. Dorrie Noble is in the back row 2nd from left.

Leeholme workers in the grounds with the Co-op in the background.

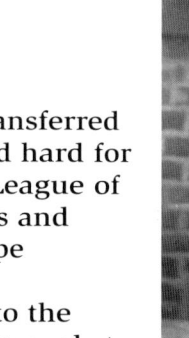

Staff at Leeholme in working clothes.

When Leeholme closed, staff and patients transferred to Ryhope Hospital. Local people had worked hard for the residents and patients and formed 'The League of Hospital Friends' to raise money for comforts and equipment for both Leeholme and Littlethorpe hospitals.

Many of the same people gave their time to the WRVS or Meals on Wheels service delivering meals to the elderly and housebound and giving them a link to the outside world.

Edna Honour and Freda Irving at Leeholme Hospital, 1955

Patients and nurses at Leeholme in 1946.

The Smallpox Hospital was at Jackson's Mill until Littlethorpe Hospital opened in 1897. A brick building was erected in 1904 originally used for infectious diseases but by the 1950s cases were so rare that Littlethorpe became the Maternity Hospital. The hospital was supported by the League of Hospital Friends who bought equipment and comforts for patients. Despite a fight by staff and local people, Thorpe was closed in 1986 and services moved to the towns and demolished in 1995. The Mill was eventually converted into a house in the 1970s (*above*).

WOMEN

A miner's wife was expected to be there to prepare the bait for both her husband and son's shifts and have meals on the table whatever the time of day. Their hard life needed good substantial food and often entire families were employed at the pit so they came home at different times – hungry, dirty and tired. Savoury puddings such as meat or leek and sweet ones with fruit from the hedgerows was a staple in all homes with food grown in the allotment where they also kept livestock for eggs and meat. Water had to be heated on the stove for the tin baths and to wash the dirty clothes, possing and mangling before ironing with a flat iron heated on the coal fire. Despite all this hard work they took a pride in keeping their homes clean. To her, events like church, clubs and groups were entertainment and a place to go to after housework.

A typical wash day with the poss tub.

Above: St Mary's Mothers' Union. Back row: Vera Smith, Eileen Laver, Elsie Walker, Ann Carter, Jane Smith, Marjorie Newby, Lorraine Dodds, Jean Forster. Front row: Doris Copeland, Audrey Brown, Kathleen Hopper, Elsie Green, Dorothy Green, Gladys Coxon, Vera Cockerham, Hazel Wilson and June Haw. The Mother's Union started in the colliery in 1917 and the village in 1925 and played an active part in village life.

Left: Easington Village Mothers' Union celebrated their 80th Birthday in 2005 and Kathleen Hopper, 97, a member for 62 years cut the cake with Branch Leader Dorothy Green.

The Women's Institute was extremely popular, with waiting lists to join their meetings, and they also had concert parties, choirs and events. It was formed in Easington Colliery in 1928 and meetings were held in the Chapel, they moved to the Welfare Hall then the Girl's Modern School when more space was needed. It closed in December 1995. Easington Village WI started in 1932 with a large membership but it also declined and closed in 1983 to be reformed in 1991 and joined by former members from the colliery and now meets in Seaton Holme.

Right: Easington Colliery WI celebrated their 34th birthday in 1962 and their oldest member Mrs Dorothy Nicholson cut the cake. They started with a membership of 20 and by 1962 had 250 members. Members were actively involved in helping local charities and in 1940 helped to feed those whose homes had been damaged in the bombing.

Left: In 1972 four Easington Colliery sisters had a combined membership of Easington Colliery Women's Institute of 104 years. Daughters of Mrs Margaret Rowcroft were Elizabeth Mason and Nora Crawford with 36 years, Nellie Sawyer with 20 years and Ethel Leadbitter with 14 years and they all served on the committee and entertainment groups.

Entertainment events were organised by both WIs. They formed drama and folk dancing groups, a choir and entertained all over the area for all ages.

Right: The Black and White Concert Party formed by Easington Colliery WI. Back: Mesdames Fiddler, ?, Williams, Cunnington, Rutherford, Wilkie. Front: Roberts, Sawyer, ?, Leadbitter.

Left: Easington Village Woman's Institute entertaining at a children's Christmas party in the church hall in 1955. Marjorie Scott is the fairy; also on the photo is Ethel Scott, Beatrice Gray and Eileen Reed but make-up stops us recognising the rest.

TURNING THE TIDE

Mining started on the east coast in the 1840s and the last pit closure on the coast was 1993 at Easington. Turning the Tide from 1997–2002 was an enormous project that received the backing of the lottery funded Millennium Commission, to remove spoil from the four pits tipping on the coast. At its height 2.5 million tonnes of waste were tipped each year by the pits totalling over 40 million tonnes of waste altogether.

Durham's beaches looked so grim that they were used as film locations in Get Carter and Alien[3].

The project won an award in recognition of the environmental improvements completed along 18km of what was one of the UK's most neglected coastlines.

To celebrate, the Sea of Lights event was held in 2000 to a synchronised display of fireworks to local singer Jez Lowe's specially commissioned music

The newly designated Durham Heritage Coast awarded in 2002 is an attractive coastal landscape of magnesian limestone grasslands, cliffs, pebble and sandy beaches stretching between the two main conurbations of Tyne and Wear and Teesside and work is still ongoing.

The aerial flight at Easington tipping colliery waste onto the shore.

These two photos show the depth of the waste left on the beach banks. Even though there was a backwash of small coal with the tide it was still a popular place to fish.

Two views of the aerial flight showing the blackened shore. The small sea coal washed back on the beach had a commercial value and men collected it in sacks to sell and wheeled it up on old bikes. Later lorries came down to the beach to collect the coal and caused even more damage to the beach.

After the top waste was removed the tide helped clear the rest and sand started to re-appear.

DURHAM HERITAGE COAST

Durham Heritage Coast was the winner of the first ever UK Landscape of Year award in November 2010. It hosts 92 per cent of the total area of para-maritime Magnesian Limestone grassland habitat in Britain. It has a unique and chequered history that has shaped the cultural identity of local communities. From Sunderland to Hartlepool, the Durham Heritage Coast has emerged from its industrial past to become one of the finest coastlines in England. Where previously colliery waste was tipped onto the beach in enormous quantities, a coastal path now leads you through a wonderful landscape mosaic of great natural, historical and geological interest with dramatic views along the coastline and out across the North Sea. The Magnesian Limestone Plateau of East Durham was laid down during the Permian period, 240 million years ago. It is formed from the remains of the skeletal structures and shells of countless animals that built reefs or settled on the bed of a tropical sea. Leading from the car park the path to the pit cage shows a geological time line of tablets sunk into the ground giving visitors some idea of the depth of the shaft, the names of the seams such as Seggar, Girdles and Coal Pipes.

The south shaft of Easington Colliery was 1586 feet (483 metres) deep. It was the main entrance for miners who reached its depths in just over a minute from the surface riding in a similar three-tier pit cage as the one shown here. Set up as a monument, the cage was shot blasted and painted in Sheffield. It weighs almost 12 tonnes and incorporates a time capsule provided by the people of Easington as a store of their memories of the local coal industry.

VILLAGE SHOW & FAIR

The Easington Village Agricultural and Horticultural Society started in 1943 and used different fields each year as the crops were cut until rising costs forced it to close in the 1960s. It was a large event with agricultural and decorated horses, pit ponies, cattle, horse jumping, dogs, cats, rabbits, pigeons, poultry and competitions for horticultural produce, handicrafts and home baking. There were eight silver challenge cups and they had record gates in 1959 with 9,000 people.

Right: Mr W. Siggens wins the cup in the Flower Class, Mrs M. Calderbank of Shotton with the Douglas Cup for onions, Mrs E. Dryden, 80, achieved her aim by winning both the Handicraft and Industrial section trophies and Mr G.W. Forbes with his prizewinning Ayreshire.

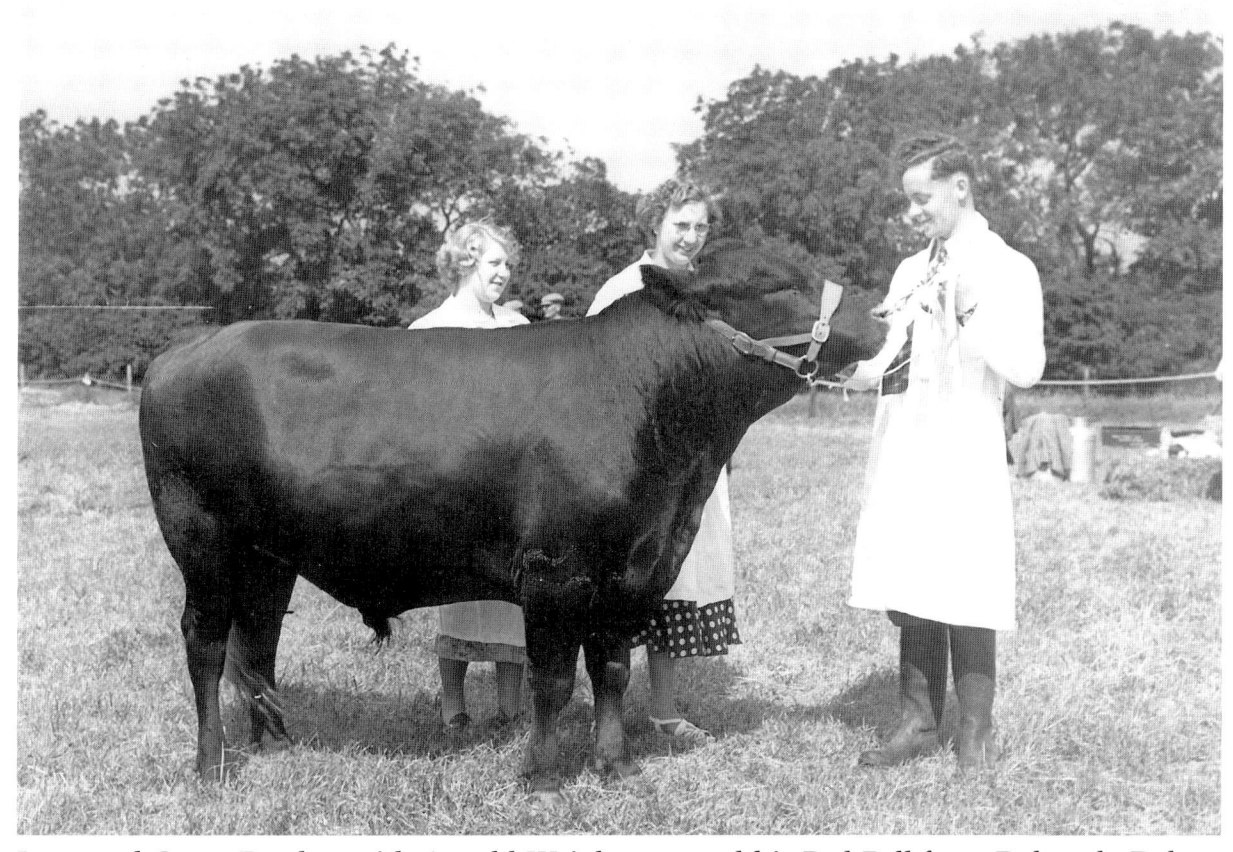

Lucy and Grace Dryden with Arnold Weightman and his Red Poll from Dalton-le-Dale.

Right: Gladys Watson and Grace Dryden with John Cowan and his Clydesdale horse from Long Cowton.

In 1980 Easington Village Residents Association looking back to the old days started in a smaller way with the Village Fair in the Comprehensive School in Stockton Road using both part of the building and the grounds. Funds went to the new car park and gardens around the old church hall. When the new parish council started, the Fair moved to Seaton Holme with less of the outdoor events, the last one was held in 1996.

Right: Farewell to Christine Dunn – Secretary of Easington Village Residents Association. Back: Christine Walker, Norman Dunn, Mavis Burn, Alice Milburn, Eileen Hopper, Ken Rowden, Ann & Steve Harrison, Tony Elgey and Vera Peacock. Front: Christine Dunn, Gillian Parker and Allen Milburn.

Left: In 1984, organisers Loraine Dodds, Alice Milburn, Mavis Burn and Gillian Parker with some of the trophies.

Jack Dormand MP with Richard Parker who entered the boys' fancy dress, at the first Village Fair, 1980.

Guides with the Roll a Penny sideshow to raise funds.

Left: As well as the races for children there was Wellie Hoying, Crate Stacking, Egg Throwing and Tug of War. Local charities and groups had stalls to raise funds.

Right: Helping out in 1985 are Stephanie Parker, Lisa Forster, Lorraine Dodds, Mavis Burn, Nicholas Parker and Eileen Hopper.

PEOPLE

To the once rural area came a great change with the coming of coal. People came from all over the country to work at the mines bringing with them their families not only from Durham but as far away as Cornwall or Ireland. As one pit closed they moved to another, men who'd worked at the lead or tin mines all helped start this new community. They needed the extra facilities for the growing community and these were built over the years. Almost everything could be bought in the colliery and people still remember the names of the old shops where they bought food, pit clothes, ladies and gents wear and sweets before going to one of the three cinemas.

Right: Arthur Bartholomew was presented to the Queen as one of the three survivors of the disaster of 1951. He celebrated his 65th wedding anniversary with his wife Vera, who he met in an air raid shelter, with his family at their home in Byron Street. They had four sons and a daughter, with 10 grandchildren and further generations.

In 1999 Tyne Tees dramatised the story of four generations of Easington women and how they faced their problems of life in the mining community. Gladys Morland, 88, with grandson Matthew Robson on her knee is shown with Melanie Robson, 23, Lynda Smith, 44 and Monica Robinson, 68.

It was the end of the line for Barbers Hardware store in 2009 after 78 years in business. Len Barber followed his father George when leaving school 48 years before but the closure of the pit and banks in the village made a difference to trade.

More and more shops have closed over the years despite the Easington Colliery Regeneration Partnership programme to improve the main roads and shop fronts.

Right: Mechanic's Trip in 1928, there are very few woman there and most of the men are wearing caps.

Left: The Easington Lodge banner at the Durham Miners' Gala passes the Royal County Hotel. The black drapes on the banner denote a death at the pit.

Right: A dance in the Welfare Hall; names in no order: Mesdames Maddison, Smith, Margaret Straughn, Audrey Bromless, Reed, Robinson, Carr, Curragh & Marjorie, Maddison, Gorley, Mavis Littler, Doris ?, Ruth Pye, E. Shanks, M. Cunnington, Audrey and Billy Kirkbride. Other men are Billy Smallwood and George Vickers.

The Frain family with the two boys Michael and Patrick and the girls Kate, Nora, Mary, Ellen, Margaret and the youngest Veronica.

Patrick Frain, an Irish miner, came to Easington from Hetton-le-Hole in 1905 with his family and eight children. After he married his wife Ellen in 1887 their first two children were born in Hebburn and Gosforth and from 1892 in Hetton. Many stayed in the area and their descendents are spread around the district.

Tommy Garside's family came to Easington in 1913 to work in the mines and Tommy and his five brothers worked underground. He started in 1920 at 14 working with a pit pony and was at the pit for 51 years followed by his five sons, the eldest was killed in the mining disaster of 1951 aged 20.

1959 – Frains from left to right: Veronica, Nora, Margaret, Patrick, Cousin Patrick, Ellen, Kate and Mary.

Barney McAndrew and Nobby Frain in 1957 – both lads worked in farming.

Gloria, Norma and Anita Scott, their father ran a fruit shop on Seaside Lane from 1953 until the mid 1970s. Both Gloria and Norma worked in the shop, later taken over by Norma's husband George Mills, Anita became a teacher and married Roy Sanderson.

Kitty, Simon, Lucy, Nollie, Bessie, Hugh and Florrie Dryden at Moor House. The two sons farmed at Moor House and Low Ling Close following their ancestors who came from Haltwhistle around 1800.

Jack Hopper (top left corner) and others at Tuthill Quarry, Haswell. I think they are wearing ARP uniforms.

The Dryden children with their donkey cart.

Stuart Hutchinson whose family farmed at Junction House.

Above: Boys after leading the greyhounds at the Moorfield dog track. Included are: Arthur Laver, George Defty, Terry Archer and Brian Bee.

Right: Miss Beatrice Delanoy born 1883 was a music teacher in Easington. She was the daughter of a joiner and her brother started the local undertaker's business and she married Joseph Tate a farmer's son.

THE FAME GAME

Easington over the years has had its share of well known people in all walks of life and odd claims to fame, a few are mentioned below.

BILLY ELLIOT

The miners' strike of 1984-5 provided the backdrop to Stephen Daldry's 2000 hit film Billy Elliot with Jamie Bell (*right*) as the child star who played Billy. Easington with its rows of back-to-back houses provided the perfect setting for the streets where he danced, and the community facing the bitter pressures of the strike. Alnwick Street featured in one of the most famous scenes in the award-winning film was bulldozed. The hit film became a West End musical and opened in 2005 with songs by Sir Elton John. In April 2010 Billy Elliot came home to perform in the Miners' Hall as part of the Billy Youth Theatre organised by Shotton Hall Theatre School and played to full house for four nights with wonderful moving performances.

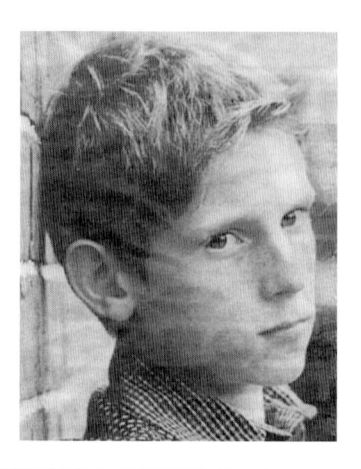

The Arthur Scargill wall specially made for the film and extras, taking the part of police in the strike, resting.

JEZ LOWE

Jez Lowe, born 1955, is a singer-songwriter. He performs both as a solo artist and with his backing band, The Bad Pennies, playing their songs and music of Northern England around the folk festivals, clubs and concert stages of the world. His songs reflect the struggles of the working class, the plight of the coal mining community and the traditional music of the North East. Jez was recently described as North East England's chief ambassador for folk music, a title deserved by many people, he insists. He began his month long US tour in July 2011 at Old Songs Festival on the East Coast of America, with an appearance at Middlebury Festival in Vermont then headed west to the California World Fest then off to Canada. He then toured England, Holland and Spain.

His father John worked in the pit for 50 years and the song 'Cursed is the Caller' is based on his father being woken by the caller to go on the first shift.

Jez Lowe by Kathryn Potts.

Who's that knocking there, who's that rapping there?
Who's that tapping there, can't you let us be.
We've been to work today, digging our lives away.
Down below the frozen clay and out beneath the sea.
Oh cursed be the caller with his knock, knock, knock.

FOOTBALL STARS

Gordon Bradley was a pioneer of US soccer (1933–2008). He went from being a coalminer and lower-league football player to a career as one of the most successful coaches in the United States. Hired by New York Cosmos, he brought in stars such as the Brazilian legend Pelé and German Franz Beckenbauer, drawing capacity crowds to the Giants' Stadium.

Alan Brown, born 1959, a useful forward, made 113 league appearances in six years for Sunderland and his son Chris later played for the club.

Adam Johnson, born 1987, went to Easington Community School and started his footballing career at Middlesbrough as a winger. He started playing for England Under-19s in 2006 moving up into the England squad in 2010.

Steve Harper was born in 1975 and attended schools in Easington. In 1993 he was signed by Newcastle United. He signed a new contract in January 2009, keeping him at the club until 2012.

MATT BAKER

Matt Baker was born in 1977 and lived near the Village Green. He trained in gymnastic and sports acrobatics and became a British champion. He later moved to the Durham dales with his family and went to drama school in Edinburgh and his first TV job was in Blue Peter. In 1999 Matt visited Easington Village C of E Primary School, where he began his education in 1982, to produce a Blue Peter Christmas Bring and Buy sale to raise cash for premature babies.

He left Blue Peter in 2006 and has since made numerous TV appearances where he often mentions his childhood.

A surprise appearance was Matt and Aliona Vilani in Strictly Come Dancing in 2010 where they were the runners up.

In May 2011, Countryfile and One Show presenter Matt was elected president of Young Farmers' Club.

Right: Competition time with the British Gymnastic Squad in 1990.

Matt enjoying the snow on the Village Green.

KEN ROWDEN

Ken Rowden was born in Horden in 1935 but spent most of his adult life in Easington and trained as an industrial welder and plater in Hartlepool shipyards. At first sculpting was a hobby until his wife Thelma encouraged him to take it up professionally in 1985. Using the crafts from his work he created unique steel sculptures and exhibited in art galleries. Many famous people across the world owned his work including Blue Peter and the Royal Shakespeare company. He died at the age of 64 and the next year one of his dearest wishes came true when a retrospective exhibition of his work was held in Seaton Holme.

CATHERINE JORDAN

Royal Navy Officer Lieutenant Commander Catherine Jordan (née Maley) of the Navy's Fishery Protection Vessel, HMS *Severn* is one of only two women in command of an operational warship in the Royal Navy. She is the elder daughter of June and Bede and attended Easington Village Primary School and with her sister, Claire was a regular at Easington's Brownies and Girl Guides. She won an academic scholarship to study at Gordonstoun School and joined the Royal Navy straight from school as a University Cadet Entrant and was offered full sponsorship through University as a Naval Aviator. She spent some time at sea before training as a helicopter observer in Lynx Helicopters. She became a Flight Commander, the first female to hold that appointment and has taken part in NATO anti-terrorism operations deployed all over the world.

In 2010 HMS *Severn*, which was featured in the TV series of Sea Patrol UK, won the Offshore Patrol Vessels' Efficiency Pennant and the squadron's most coveted award – the Jersey Cup – in recognition of their work and also won the Squadron Sport's Day.

JOE SAVAGE

Joe Savage, a former Easington Village resident, died in Yohden Dene Care Home in 2009 at the age of 109 and was Britain's second oldest man as well as the fourth oldest man in Europe. He started work aged 14 as an errand boy and eventually became a Sanitary Inspector, a Chief Officer for Health for County Durham and was one of the first River Inspectors for the Wear and Tees River Board. He was involved with the church, the Parish Council and was the local Labour Party Chairman. One of the first with a movie camera he filmed scenes of events in the village many years ago. He and his wife Mona, who died in 1994, had two children, seven grandchildren, 16 great-grandchildren and a great-great grandchild.

Right: Joe and his family as he is presented with a birthday cake from Asda store.

EASINGTON SAGA IN VERSE

In 2007 residents of Easington were enthralled by a series of verses remembering times, people and places of their youth. The first verse was published in the Church of the Ascension Times magazine in May and copies were hard to get. Then in June and July other people sent in follow-ups with further information and it became a local talking point.

Does the village church still stand
Above the Green on hallowed land
Does Rosemary Lane still tumble down
From Masons Arms to Lion House and stout Jack Brown

Does Seaside Lane still take the load
From Kings Head to Station Road
Past Leeholme Hospital and Murton store
Does Willie Hewitson still operate as before

Does Miss Best still rule the Senior Girls
And Mr Suffield disperse such pearls
Can 40 lads, or even more, still be seen
Playing football on the Big Club green

Does the Rialto still have Daisy there
Selling tickets to films beyond compare
And the Hippodrome not quite so good
Where Errol Flynn played Robin Hood

Does Hanley's pease pudding still pass the test
Does his sausages still beat all the best
Is Barbers hardware shop still there
Does sleek Jack Calvert still cut hair

Do they still dance at the Miners' Hall
Does Gilbert Ridley's band still play them all
Does Tommy Reynolds still blow the horn
From eight o'clock till early morn

Does Equi's Café de luxe still exist
The first juke box who could resist
Tuppence a record the price to pay
Sinatra, Elvis and Doris Day

Is Nashies billiard hall still there
And Atkins corner for all menswear
Does Mary Lizzie still fry fish and chips
Taste of vinegar on the lips

Do we still have Ryhope store
Is Scott's fruit shop still next door
Do the daughters still walk out in Summer dresses
Lovely girls with raven tresses

Does jovial Duncan still supply
The incomparable Burdess's pie
Does Mr Ferry still dispense for one and all
From tiny window in the rear wall

Does the pit canteen still serve at any hour
The mighty meals the lads devour
Does South still stand and along the top
Bede Street from Walter Willsons to Donnelly's shop

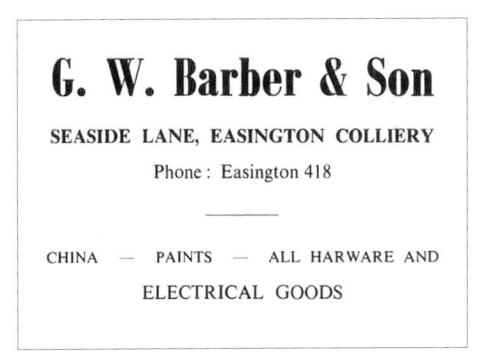

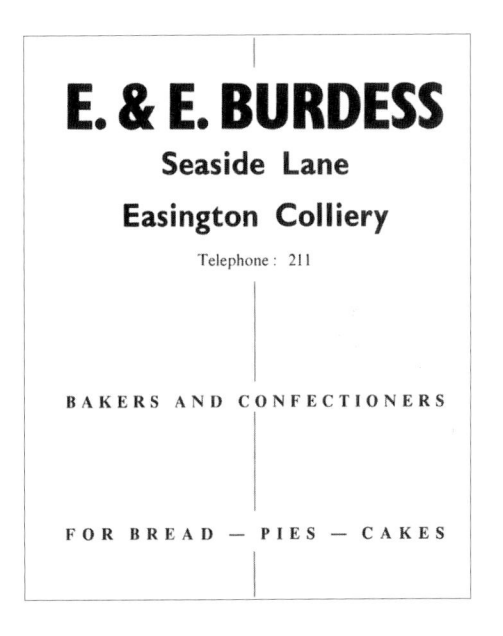

RIALTO, Easington.
Continuous from 6 p.m.   Sunday 8 p.m.

Oct 7, 8, 9. Dean Martin, Lana Turner in
WHO'S GOT THE ACTION   A
also
WARPATH   U

Oct 10, 11, 12. John Wayne,
Hardy Kruger, Elsa Martinelli in
HATARI   U

Oct 13 (Sun.) Robert Wagner,
Dana Wynter in
IN LOVE AND WAR   A

G. W. Barber & Son

SEASIDE LANE, EASINGTON COLLIERY

Phone: Easington 418

CHINA — PAINTS — ALL HARWARE AND
ELECTRICAL GOODS

E. & E. BURDESS

Seaside Lane

Easington Colliery

Telephone: 211

BAKERS AND CONFECTIONERS

FOR BREAD — PIES — CAKES

Does Harold Milburn still scrub the block
Does Reverend Beddoes still tend his flock
Does the Church of the Ascension still remain
Most welcoming sight on Seaside Lane

Should I go on and bore you more
With memories of days of yore
How many characters have I missed
Who would you add to this list

Do you remember so much better
Then why not answer by phone or letter
Your memories of days gone by
That we may all enjoy that inward eye.

EVEN MORE QUESTIONS (and a conclusion)

Does Miss Wardell still run the Infant girls
Shy dimpled faces, ringlets, curls
Does Miss Ruddock still welcome the Infant boys
Does Mr Galley still sell the toys

Does Jack Dawson still tend the Big Club bars
Does Norman Pearce still sell the cars
Does George Cole still book the back row seats
Does Blanche Wragg still sell the sweets

Does Charlie Passerotti still make his own ice cream
The rebuilt Empire still spin the dream
The Diamonds corner, afternoons, bookies stand
Sunday evenings, Salvation band

Does Kilgour still lock up the crooks
And Les Dryden still sort the books
Does Nessie Hart still sell the hazelnut whirls
Does Jacksons drapers still clothe the girls

Does Joe Leith still sell bikes on the never-never
Rent out TV sets – pay for ever
Does Bunty Robinson still deliver the news
And Dusty Birkbeck sells the screws

Does old R H Appleby still sort the post
Dewhirsts butchers supply the roast
Fresh killed meat from Bede Street Milburns
Kit out Guides and Scouts at Kilburns

Is the Waterworks still there
Chimneys towering in the air
Do they still misspend their youth in the billiard hall
Trying to sink the last black ball

Did Easington breed those mining men
Never see their like again
Not all were good, not all were just
But all were brave for that's a must
To slave in muck and poisonous dust
Their time is past, their day is done
Let us revere them, everyone.

Shop at

KILBURNS

HORDEN, Co. DURHAM

For—
- OUTERWEAR
- UNDERWEAR
- FOOTWEAR and
- HOUSEHOLD GOODS

Where—
you will be offered a good and varied selection, with courtesy and every attention to your requirements

★

Branches at

**BLACKHALL, EASINGTON
SHOTTON & SOUTH HETTON**

NEWSAGENTS   STATIONERY
JEWELLERY . ORNAMENTS

A. ROBINSON

2 SEASIDE LANE, EASINGTON COLLIERY

Phone : Easington 257

Excellent Selection of Greetings Cards
STOCKISTS OF ALL TRIANG TOYS

N.C.B.

COAL

By its ability both in efficiency and economy to meet all the needs of the modern age, Coal still reigns supreme. Available in grades suitable for all requirements, in consistent quality and sufficient quantity to meet even the largest demand. Coal is today, even more than ever before, the fuel for modern industry. Used in up-to-date appliances Coal is smokeless, meeting all the requirements of the Clean Air Act.

To help users obtain full value from every ton of Coal, the N.C.B. offers a free advisory service by highly experienced fuel technologists, qualified to answer any problem associated with the use of solid fuels.

THE ANSWERS I GIVE

Yes we still have church and green
Mason's Arms may still be seen
Rosemary Lane still tumbles down
Look in vain for Lion House and Mr Brown

Best and Suffield beyond recall
Modern school felt the wrecking ball
Big Club Green reserved for motors
No ball games proclaims the notice

The Hippodrome, alas no more
The Rialto, carpets for the floor
To see Errol, Ingrid and cool Grace Kelly
Stay at home and watch the telly

Mister Hanley dead and gone
Lenny Barbers soldiers on
No Tot Williams in trilby hat
No billiard hall, remember Matty

Jack Calvert no longer snips
No Sumner's shop nor bran tub dips
Miners' Hall still there for dancing
Sadly no Tom or Gilbert to help their prancing

Equi, Nashie and Mary Lizzie
All now keeping the good Lord busy
Mr Ferry, the dispensary in the skies
Duncan, retired from baking the pies

Bede Street still runs along the top
No more Walter Willsons or Donnelly's shop
And South from Bradley to Baldwin Street
Demolition all too complete

Harold Milburn now scrubs heaven's block
Reverend Close inherits the flock
The colliery church does still remain
One uplifting sight on Seaside Lane

Yes we have lost Ryhope store
And Scotts fruit shop from next door
The daughters remaining two are fine
One of them has long been mine.

THANK YOU MYSTERY WRITER EVERYONE ENJOYED YOUR MEMORIES.

Part of it was Roy Sanderson and he gave permission to use the verses.

J. N. BROWN

Newsagent, Stationer and Tobacconist

CONFECTIONERY, MINERALS & ICE CREAM
FANCY GOODS — LENDING LIBRARY

Newspapers Delivered in Easington Village
and Easington Colliery

Albion House, Easington Village

Gentlemen . . .

for a First-Class Show

TRY

OPEN DAILY
9 a.m. till 6 p.m.
TUESDAYS
9 a.m. till 12 noon

CALVERTS

GENT'S HAIRDRESSER

SEASIDE LANE
EASINGTON COLLIERY

Special attention given to Children!

Family Grocers since 1875

WALTER WILLSON LTD.

EASINGTON VILLAGE

OUR MOTTO

Smiling Service   Civility and Satisfaction

Shop at the . . .

Murton Colliery Co-operative Society

------ Limited ------

For everything you require in

FURNITURE, CARPETS
FANCY GOODS
Gowns Millinery Drapery
Boots, Shoes & Groceries
ETC.

ACKNOWLEDGEMENTS

I would like to thank all those who loaned photos and gave information and shared their memories with me. They were not only given locally but sent from people who moved away, even as far as Canada. I apologise for pestering people for names on the photos, my friends who have taken copies to show others and all the help I have been given. Many thanks to my husband's friends at Easington Colliery Big Club who poured over the sporting photos and my husband John for all the running about he has done on my behalf. Every care has been taken to ensure the information is accurate but memory is not always exact and it was thought to be correct at the time of printing.

We thank the Sunderland Echo and Hartlepool Mail and other local papers for the use of their articles, many of them saved on my local history files over the years and a good source of dating events.

Blackpool was a favourite place for holidays for Easington folk and here is a happy group who stayed at some of the boarding houses in the famous seaside resort.

Summerhill Books

Summerhill Books publishes local history books in Northumberland, Durham and Tyneside. To receive a free catalogue send a SAE envelope to:

Summerhill Books, PO Box 1210, Newcastle NE99 4AH

or email: summerhillbooks@yahoo.co.uk

or visit our website to view the full range of titles

www.summerhillbooks.co.uk

Postage and packaging is FREE for all UK orders.